trotman

GUIDES

THE FIRE SERVICE

Dee Pilgrim

Real Life Guide to the Fire Service
This first edition published in 2006 by Trotman and Company Ltd
2 The Green, Richmond, Surrey TW9 1PL

Editorial and Publishing Team
Author Dee Pilgrim
Editorial Mina Patria, Editorial Director; Jo Jacomb, Editorial
Manager; Catherine Travers, Managing Editor; Ian Turner,
Editorial Assistant
Production Ken Ruskin, Head of Pre-press and Production
Sales and Marketing Suzanne Johnson, Marketing Manager
Advertising Tom Lee, Commercial Director

Designed by XAB

British Library Cataloguing in Publication Data

A catalogue record for this book is available from the British
Library

ISBN 1 84455 089 3

Typeset by Photoprint, Torquay
Printed and bound by Creative Print & Design Group, Wales

Real Life GUIDES

THE FIRE SERVICE

REAL LIFE GUIDES

Practical guides for practical people

In this increasingly sophisticated world the need for manually skilled people to build our homes, cut our hair, fix our boilers and to make our cars go is greater than ever. As things progress, so the level of training and competence required of our skilled manual workers increases.

In this series of career guides from Trotman, we look in detail at what it takes to train for, get into, and be successful at a wide spectrum of practical careers. The *Real Life Guides* aim to inform and inspire young people and adults alike by providing comprehensive yet hard-hitting and often blunt information about what it takes to succeed in these careers.

Other titles in the series are:

Real Life Guide: The Armed Forces
Real Life Guide: The Beauty Industry
Real Life Guide: Carpentry and Cabinet-Making
Real Life Guide: Catering
Real Life Guide: Construction
Real Life Guide: Distribution and Logistics
Real Life Guide: Electrician
Real Life Guide: The Fire Service
Real Life Guide: Hairdressing
Real Life Guide: The Motor Industry
Real Life Guide: The Police Force
Real Life Guide: Plumbing
Real Life Guide: Retailing
Real Life Guide: Transport
Real Life Guide: Working Outdoors
Real Life Guide: Working with Animals and Wildlife
Real Life Guide: Working with Young People

Real
Life

GUIDES

CONTENTS

About the author

Dee Pilgrim studied journalism at the London College of Printing before working on a variety of music and women's titles. As a freelancer and a full-time member of staff she has written numerous articles and interviews for *Company*, *Cosmopolitan*, *New Woman*, *Woman's Journal* and *Weight Watchers* magazines. As a freelancer for Independent Magazines she concentrated on celebrity interviews and film, theatre and restaurant reviews for such titles as *Ms London*, *Girl About Town*, *LAM* and *Nine to Five* magazines, and in her capacity as a critic she has appeared on both radio and television. She is currently the Film Reviewer for *Now* magazine. When not attending film screenings she is active within the Critics' Circle, co-writes songs and is currently engaged in writing the narrative to an as-yet unpublished trilogy of children's illustrated books. She has written a variety of titles for Trotman Publishing including four other titles in the Real Life Guides series.

Acknowledgements

Thanks are due to both Alex Dunnet, Area Manager for Training and Development, and Robert Winyard, the Group Manager, Head of Access and Development, at Kent Fire and Emergency Services for their input into the 'Training Day' chapter of this book. Thanks must also go to Deborah Aniyeloye who supplied all the information and statistics on the fire services from the Department of Communities and Local Government, and to Gemma Green for her input re. the Forensic Fire Service. Finally, thank-you to the actual firefighters who agreed to be interviewed for the Case Studies in this book: Rob Line, Jim Gill and Carly Taylor – all great examples of what it takes to be a successful firefighter.

Introduction

BACKGROUND

The siren's wail and the flash of emergency lights as a big red fire truck rushes past always manage to turn heads. It's an image we associate with danger and excitement and urgency. We think of firefighters as heroes, voluntarily putting their own lives on the line in order to save others. They venture into burning buildings, help cut people free from crashed cars, give assistance during flooding, attend and contain chemical spills, and during the London terrorist bombings even administered first aid to victims. In fact, there is such an allure attached to the job of firefighter, as portrayed in films such as *Ladder 49* and on television in series such as *London's Burning*, positions for trainee firefighters are always vastly oversubscribed with over 40 applications for each place.

A VARIED JOB

However, the truth of the matter is that for all the excitement, a firefighter's job can also be grubby, grimy and perilous. It can also be emotionally distressing when the people you have set out to save fail to make it. In fact, emergency call-outs (known in the trade as 'shouts') take up only a small part of a firefighter's time. While at the station they will be doing much more mundane – although essential – tasks such as checking equipment and receiving training, or they may be out in the community advising on fire safety and fitting fire alarms, or they could even be rescuing people trapped in lifts or other confined spaces. So, it's not all glamorous, adrenalin-fuelled stuff. However, our modern fire service is extremely professional and well equipped with the most up to date technology, and offers those who work within it satisfying and varied careers that can bring new experiences each and every day.

A TIME OF CHANGE

Every year, in the UK over 33,000 wholetime (full-time) firefighters, and 12,000 retained (part-time) firefighters respond to more than 60,000 accidental house fires and 72,000 vehicle fires. But the challenges a modern firefighter faces no longer begin and end with actually putting fires out. The job remit has changed enormously in the last few years and much of the change was sparked off by the national fire strike that took place at the end of 2002 and early 2003 (read more about the strike in the next chapter). This in turn led to the government's White Paper 'Our Rescue and Fire Service' which set up the blueprint for the fire and rescue service of the future and finally resulted in the Fire and Rescue Services Act published in 2004. It is this new Act that is pushing forward just what it means to be a firefighter in the modern world, where our fire and rescue services not only have to respond to local challenges but also to the threat of national acts of terror, such as organising mass decontamination after a nuclear or chemical weapons attack, or to coping with huge emergencies such as the Buncefield oil depot explosions and fire in Hertfordshire. Another aspect of the firefighter's work being highlighted by the Act is fire prevention with the government determined to reduce the number of deaths by accidental fire by 20%, and by arson by 10%, by 2010.

Every year, in the UK over 33,000 wholetime (full-time) firefighters, and 12,000 retained (part-time) firefighters respond to more than 60,000 accidental house fires and 72,000 vehicle fires.

Because of this the way firefighters are trained is changing and if you are seriously thinking of joining the fire and rescue services these changes will directly affect you. Alex Dunnet is the Area Manager for Training and Development at Kent Fire and Emergency Services. He says:

'The aim of the changes has been to get better quality applicants. The reality is this is a highly technical job. You need some practical skills, some technical skills and you need some academic skills depending on whichever role you are working at. We need rounded people to do this and our job as trainers is to attract the very best applicants for that. Getting into the job now is extremely difficult and doing the initial training is much more challenging and a much tougher process than when I did it.'

This book will concentrate on the new learning programmes being implemented throughout 2006 and 2007, especially the introduction of the Integrated Personal Development System (IPDS) which offers a continuous training programme while on the job, to ensure each individual reaches his or her full potential. 'Traditionally we have had a single tier entry system so it has taken a long time to come through the service to reach officer level,' says Alex. 'Now, individuals can come in and be assessed and those with potential will be fast-tracked so they can move through the ranks more easily.'

DID YOU KNOW?

The Disability Rights Commission has produced a guidance document which provides the UK fire service with advice on the implementation of Part 2 of the Disability Discrimination Act 1995. For further information see: www.drc-gb.org.

At present the stereotypical view of a firefighter as being a muscular white male still holds true with 97.9% being male and 95.2% being white, but the government has pledged to draw members of the fire and rescue services from a wider pool in the future. It has set targets of achieving 15% women in operational roles and 7% ethnic minorities as a percentage of the total workforce by 2009.

INTERESTED?

Do you have the talents and skills to be part of that team? More importantly, would you want to be in a job where you never know what the next hour will bring, let alone the next month? This is why this book exists. It will tell you what being a firefighter is really like, warts and all. It will also explain what qualifications or attributes you need to apply, what the selection process is like, and what you will actually do during your training. It will also tell you just how far up the promotional ladder you can climb – if you really want to.

If you've picked this book up in the first place it means you must have some interest, however fleeting, in what the fire and rescue services actually do. Now read on to see if this challenging, competitive and potentially lifelong career is for you, and if you have what it takes to be a success in the fire and rescue services.

FIRE JARGON BOX

Wholetime firefighter A person employed full-time as a firefighter regardless of their rank.

Retained duty system (RDS) firefighter Basically, a part-time firefighter. A person who contracts to be available for agreed periods of time for firefighting purposes, but who could have an alternative full-time employment.

Fire control staff Uniformed personnel who are employed to work in fire and rescue service control centres to answer emergency calls.

Non-uniformed staff Generally support/administrative staff employed by a Fire and Rescue Authority (FRA).

Operational personnel Staff who attend, or could be required to attend, incidents.

Appliance A fire and rescue service vehicle that attends an incident.

Attendance Predetermined resources mobilised to an incident, based upon risk analysis.

HAZMAT Hazardous materials (combustible chemicals etc).

Integrated personal development system (IPDS) A new training, development and assessment system for Fire and Rescue Service (FRS) personnel based on role, not rank.

Shout The firefighters' name for an emergency call-out.

Protective personal equipment (PPE) The fireproof suit, face protection and breathing apparatus issued to firefighters.

Watch (eg Blue Watch, Green Watch etc). The name given to a group of firefighters working together as a unit/team.

What's the story?

1

HOW IT ALL STARTED

Watching the professional way the fire services handle accidents and emergencies these days, it's almost impossible to believe that at one stage Britain had no way to deal with fires however big or small. As is so often the case, it took an incident of huge proportions to change all that and that incident is known as the Great Fire of London of 1666. There had been a previous fire of London in 1212 and as most of the buildings at that time were made of timber and other combustible substances it had done a lot of damage; upwards of 3000 people were killed. However, this was nothing compared to the Great Fire in 1666 which started in Pudding Lane, at the home of the King's Baker, and went on to destroy 12,000 houses, leaving 200,000 people homeless as it raged out of control for three days. Unbelievably, only six people were known to die in the blaze but the chaos and misery it caused forced the authorities to think seriously about fire prevention.

DID YOU KNOW?

The Great Fire of London 1666 destroyed the following:

- 13,200 houses
- St Paul's Cathedral
- 87 parish churches
- 6 chapels
- Bridewell Prison
- Newgate Prison
- The Guildhall
- 3 City gates
- The Custom House
- 4 stone bridges
- Sessions House
- The Royal Exchange
- 52 livery company hall

Source
Museum of London
(www.museumoflondon.org.uk)

So, householders were charged an 'insurance premium' to cover the cost of fires and had plaques on the front of their buildings showing they had paid. Thus the first 'insurance fire brigades' were born with the City being divided into quarters with each quarter getting its own fire equipment.

PROGRESSION

Gradually, technology was introduced and in 1721 a pump that could supply an efficient continuous clean jet of water was developed. In 1832 several of the London insurance companies amalgamated, and a certain James Braidwood was recruited as head of the London Fire Engine Establishment. His input as far as organising men and establishing discipline was enormous, but sadly he died while attending a fire in 1861. However, the fledgling fire brigades continued to evolve; a Metropolitan police fire brigade was formed in 1866 and many local brigades followed shortly after. The problem was they all used different equipment so hose fittings from some areas were not compatible with the standpipes from others rendering them useless. Things didn't really change until the onset of the Second World War when it became obvious a unified service was needed and on 22nd May 1941 the National Fire Service (NFS) was formed, linking up firefighting services throughout the country. The NFS was instrumental in converting most hydrants to the standard sluice valve type and standardised other equipment as well, but it was gradually disbanded after the war.

THE MODERN FIRE SERVICE

In 1947 the Fire Services Act of Parliament was passed stating the purpose of firefighters was to save life, to protect property from damage by fire and to render humanitarian services. On 1st April 1948 firefighting was returned to local authority control from the NFS. More legislation was passed in 1956 after a fire at a mill in Keighley, Yorkshire, to cover fire safety at work, and in April 1974 large County brigades were formed, losing the old City and County Boroughs.

However, the recent massive changes to the fire and emergency services as we know them came about because of the firefighters' strike in 2002. The Fire Brigades' Union (FBU) was unwilling to accept reforms contained in the Independent Review of the Fire Services (IRFS), which had been headed by Sir George Blain, and also rejected his pay recommendations. After a series of strikes across the country an agreement was finally reached in 2003 when the FBU accepted working methods must be overhauled in order for the fire services to be able to deal efficiently with modern day situations. Thus, on 1st October 2004, the Fire and Rescue Services Act came into being, replacing the 1947 Act.

FIRE AND RESCUE SERVICES ACT 2004 (1ST OCTOBER)

- Promoting community fire safety is at the heart of the role of the fire and rescue services.
- Greater emphasis is placed on fire prevention that will help save more lives and reduce injuries from fire. This is one of the new powers that will help the fire and rescue service to create safer communities, particularly for the most vulnerable people in society.
- The Act also formally recognises for the first time the wider roles the service has taken on over the

---

last 50 years. These go beyond firefighting duties and include rescues from road traffic accidents, responding to serious environmental disasters such as flooding and the new terrorist threat. The Fire and Rescue Services Act 2004 replaces the Fire Services Act 1947 and will drive forward the Government's modernisation agenda to create a modern and efficient Fire and Rescue Service designed to meet the challenges of the twenty-first century.

Source: Department of Communities and Local Government (DCLG)

Now our fire services are better equipped with better-trained personnel than ever before. There are 62 separate fire services in England, Wales, Scotland and Northern Ireland and the islands of Guernsey, Jersey and Scilly although these may be amalgamating into fewer but larger services in the future.

In 1947 the Fire Services Act of Parliament was passed stating the purpose of firefighters was to save life, to protect property from damage by fire and to render humanitarian services.

FIREFIGHTING ROLES
The jobs you can do within these fire services are almost as varied as the type of incidents they are called out to

(everything from farming accidents, to rescuing animals and attempted suicides – see 'Non-fire incidents' box on p 15). Not all of these jobs will have the perceived glamour of the firefighter, but they are essential if the fire services are to work efficiently. The illustration on the next page will give you an indication of where they all work, while here you'll find an explanation about what they all do.

It is the job of a **firefighter** that is the most visible within the service as these are the men and women we see attending blazes and other incidents on a daily basis. In March 2004 there were 33,573 wholetime firefighters in England and Wales, while there were also 12,476 retained duty (part-time) firefighters (Source: all statistics from the DCLG). They answered calls to a staggering 509,716 fires and 42,437 road traffic incidents in the year 2003/2004. While not out on 'shouts' firefighters train, check equipment, write reports and increasingly, go into the community to talk to the public at large about fire prevention and safety. As stated earlier, until recently the training for firefighters was a one-tier system where everyone started at the same level and could climb the career ladder through further training and obtaining more experience. This has now changed with the introduction of the IPDS, which means those candidates who show the most potential will be fast-tracked through the system (this is explored in detail in the 'Training Day' chapter). The job titles given to firefighters as they go through the levels of seniority

A firefighter is the most visible within the service as these are the men and women we see attending blazes and other incidents on a daily basis.

JOBS WITHIN THE FIRE AND EMERGENCY SERVICES

FIRE AND EMERGENCY SERVICES JOB OPTIONS

AT FIRE SCENES, FIRE STATIONS AND REGIONAL HQ

AT CONTROL ROOMS

UNIFORMED FIRE CONTROL STAFF

- TAKING EMERGENCY CALLS AND DISPATCHING THE APPROPRIATE APPLIANCES (ENGINES ETC) AND PERSONNEL TO THE SCENE.
- LIAISING WITH OTHER EMERGENCY SERVICES.
- COLLATING STATISTICAL INFORMATION

FIREFIGHTERS
Retained (part-time)
DAY SHIFT (part-time)
FIREFIGHTERS (Wholetime)

- FIREFIGHTER
- CREW MANAGER
- WATCH MANAGER
- STATION MANAGER
- GROUP MANAGER
- AREA MANAGER
- BRIGADE MANAGER

OTHER ROLES

- ENGINEERING
- VEHICLE MAINTENANCE
- EQUIPMENT BUYER
- ADMINISTRATION
  - SECRETARIAL
  - ACCOUNTANCY
- IT
- TRAINING
- MANAGEMENT

FORENSIC FIRE INVESTIGATORS

WORK ROUGHLY 50/50 OF THE TIME AT FIRE SCENES AND IN LABORATORIES EXAMINING WHAT STARTED FIRES, LOOKING AT CLOTHING FOR FLASHBURNS AND IDENTIFYING FLAMMABLE LIQUIDS and responsibility are given in the list below starting with the most inexperienced rising to the most senior.

- Trainee firefighter
- Firefighter
- Crew manager
- Watch manager
- Station manager
- Group manager
- Area manager
- Brigade manager.

Firefighers are known as operational staff (they operate the fire engines and go out on operations), but elsewhere in the fire services there are numerous other **non-operational uniformed staff** who undertake other duties. These include **fire safety advisers** and **equipment operatives** (looking after breathing equipment and PPE). There are also 1556 **fire control staff** working in control centres across the country handling the literally thousands of calls the fire services receive each year. They need to remain calm while getting as much information from callers as quickly as possible. They also track appliances and co-ordinate with the other emergency services. In the extremely busy London Fire Brigade, each operator handled approximately 3207 calls in 2003/2004. Elsewhere, on the less frantic Isle of Wight, each operator handled just 252 calls.

DID YOU KNOW?

In 2003/2004, the main cause of accidental dwelling fires remained the misuse of equipment/appliances (17,200 fires), while the main source of ignition was cooking appliances (57% of all accidental dwelling fires).

Source: DCLG

There are also many **non-uniformed support staff** working in the fire services in roles as diverse as **IT, engineering, vehicle maintenance**, in **administration** such as **HR**, and **equipment buying** and performing **secretarial** duties.

Connected to the fire services, although not employed by them, are the **forensic fire investigators**. These are members of the Forensic Science Service, such as **casework reporting officers**, who undertake a further 18 months to two years of training in order to ascertain if a fire is accidental or deliberately started and if so, what was used to cause the fire. At the request of the police they visit and examine the scenes of fires, removing any evidence for further study in the laboratory. Because of the nature of the work they do most forensic fire investigators have a hard science background in chemistry, physics or engineering. (See separate box on p 61).

Obviously, what you decide to do, or what you are capable of doing, within the fire services will very much depend on your qualifications and your own strengths and weaknesses, both mental and physical. In the next chapter you'll find information on which of your personal qualities will help make you a success in this profession.

DID YOU KNOW?

In 2004, there were 508 fire-related deaths in the UK, compared with 593 in 2003. The highest number recorded was 1096 deaths in 1979. Through the 1980s and 1990s there was a general downward trend. The 2004 figure is the lowest in 45 years.

Source: DCLG

NON-FIRE INCIDENTS, 2003/2004
Road incidents total: 42,437
Persons extricated from vehicles: 10,195
Services only rendered: 26,744
No services rendered: 5498

Non-road traffic incidents total: 124,222
Spills and leaks: 11,814
Water – removal/provision: 9586
Effecting entry: 13,772
Lift releases: 26,297
Animal rescues: 5293
Other rescue/release of people: 7728
Removal of objects from people: 4334
First aid: 3869
Making safe: 7427
Recovery/retrieval of objects: 515
Standby/precautionary action: 1804
Aircraft incidents (no fire): 217
Assistance to Police and Ambulance: 4805
Industrial: 206
Sports activity: 44
Farming accidents: 37
Suicides/attempted suicides: 824
Railway accidents: 72

Provision of advice
Officer and appliance/equipment: 1771
Officer only: 2145
Use of appliance/equipment not specified: 1006

Services not required
Malicious: 1091
Good intent: 12,626
Other: 3258
Call type not known: 564
Any other special services: 3117

Total non-fire incidents: 166,659

Source: DCLG

Case study 1

2

FIREFIGHTER

In 1998, while working as a ship's joiner in Hampshire, 32-year-old Rob mentioned to a colleague he wouldn't mind being a firefighter. As it happened the colleague had seen a recruitment ad placed by Hampshire Fire Service in the local paper and so Rob went to the job centre the next day and filled in an application form. His application was accepted and he then went through a series of test days, including a physical test and ability range test, before going on to a formal interview. Having passed this Rob then spent 15 weeks on an in-house, residential course at Hampshire's training centre in Eastleigh, before joining High Town station in Southampton as a probationer. After completing his four-year probationary and training period Rob is now a firefighter at High Town. Rob also works as a Fire Safety Officer at Twickenham during rugby matches.

'I'm the kind of person who prefers to be outside rather than stuck in an office which is why I want to stay as a firefighter rather than go for promotion because I enjoy this side of things rather than having to do

> The job is different every day and you just don't know what is going to happen.

loads of paperwork. If you get on a good watch (a team of firefighters) you work well together and there's a great sense of camaraderie, it's also great when you rescue someone, say like going to a car accident and getting someone out of a crashed car. I also like the fact the job is different every day and you just don't know what is going to happen. There are plenty of courses you can go on too, for instance I now have a LGV (Light Goods Vehicle) license meaning I can drive the engine. You can also become an instructor teaching other firefighters in lots of different areas. I'm a Physical Training Instructor and also a Manual Handling Instructor.

'The downsides to the job are the fires and accidents where people die, especially children. Sometimes you want to be of help but you physically can't. There's also always a risk at any incident you go to. Although you are trained to deal with them, accidents do happen because there's a lot of lifting and moving things about but the facilities are there if you do get injured. We have our own occupational health department with our own doctor and physio, we also have a rehabilitation centre. However, I don't think about getting injured; by its nature this is a dangerous job because at the end of the day you are the person walking into a burning building while everyone else is running away, but I don't think of the risks, I am trained to do what I am doing.

'I'm not a lover of blood or body parts, other firefighters don't like working in confined spaces, while quite a few are scared of heights. But you get over it because of the really thorough training you do. This is what a watch is all about; some people are better at some things, such as casualty care, than others so you all have to work together.

'To do this job you need to be able to work as one of a team, but you also need to be able to work on your own initiative. You need to be fairly practical and you need lots of common sense.

'I'd say to anyone who may think this job is for them: just go for it because it really is enjoyable. Look at your local service's website and see if they have open days coming up. Most fire stations are quite friendly so go in and ask if they'll point you in the right direction. There are plenty of opportunities for promotion and advancement, but the service will always need experienced firefighters like myself and I'm quite happy to stay where I am and not go any higher.'

Tools of the trade

3

In today's highly competitive atmosphere you will need more than just a strong desire to get a place as a trainee firefighter. Even if it has been your ambition since you were a child, and you have good educational qualifications, you will need something extra to stand out from the other potential candidates vying to get on the training programme. For a start, a certain standard of physical fitness is obviously necessary for you to be able to do the job. However, it is other, more abstract strengths such as reasoning, logic, perception and judgement that will be your most useful 'tools' helping you to become a successful firefighter. These are what are known as your Personal Qualities and Attributes (PQAs). These are the skills that show you will be able to cope well with the pressures of being a firefighter, will be able to get on with your co-workers and with the community at large, and won't panic when faced with an emergency. Because you'll be using these tools as much, if not more than, actual hoses, sledgehammers and breathing apparatus, much of the training firefighters receive during the modern training programme reinforces these attributes. However, if you already possess them it will stand you in good stead as you go through the National Firefighter Selection process – especially at the PQA interview stage.

It's about becoming part of a team.

PHYSICAL FITNESS/GOOD EYESIGHT

Although this is a physical attribute rather than a mental one, as stated above you will need a certain level of fitness before you are even considered for training. Lifting heavy hoses and equipment, dragging unconscious bodies from buildings, and getting up and down ladders in heavy PPE (protective personal equipment) mean you need stamina and strength. You'll also need good eyesight, especially when you are working at night or when your vision is hampered by smoke. At present you need good eyesight without glasses or contact lenses, although some services will consider those who have had corrective laser surgery. You also need good colour vision. However, the guidelines are currently under revision so it pays to check with the service you are interested in joining first.

ATTITUDE

Alex Dunnet of Kent Fire and Emergency Services says 'It's all about attitude. It's about wanting to get involved in everything you do, it's about becoming part of a team and you can quickly spot people who are standing back, letting other people do everything and not putting in 110%.' So show your enthusiasm and your interest. Don't wait for others to volunteer for tasks, show you are eager to do things and to learn new skills. An outward going, positive attitude will help you get on with other trainees and trainers alike.

ABILITY TO WORK WITH OTHERS

As Alex says, in the fire service you have to work as part of a team so you need to be an outgoing, socially friendly person. You will be relying on the other members of your watch to look out for you, in the same way you have to look out for them during potentially dangerous situations. In Jim Gill's case study (Case Study 2) he admits you may sometimes fall out with your comrades while off-duty, but while on-duty you all have to pull together. You will also be dealing with members of the public on a day to day basis so, says Alex 'we want people whose skills are about interfacing with the public and who care about working in the community.'

CONFIDENCE

The modern fire service isn't looking for hot-headed heroes so much as people who have the confidence in their own ability to stay calm in hazardous situations. Hot-headed heroes have a habit of getting themselves (and others) into trouble, while those who are confident can calmly assess situations and take all necessary precautions instead of charging in regardless. A confident person instils confidence in others and stops panic from developing. So confidence is one of the key PQAs the fire service is looking for, especially those who are prime candidates for the IPDS (Integrated Personal Development System).

The modern fire service isn't looking for hot-headed heroes so much as people who have the confidence in their own ability to stay calm in hazardous situations.

GOOD COMMUNICATION SKILLS

You've been called to a house fire where people are still trapped in the dwelling. It's night, it's loud and people are panicking. Not only do you need to make yourself understood quickly and efficiently, you also need to be able to understand orders as soon as they are given. Good communication skills can save lives. However, these days the fire services are looking for people who can not only communicate effectively orally, but also in writing as there are many reports you will have to complete during your daily routine. If you don't think your writing skills are up to scratch this is an area you can really work on before undergoing the selection process by keeping your own daily diary and checking your entries are clear, precise and easily understood.

COMMON SENSE

If you are a daydreamer who always has your head in the clouds you are going to find the realities of being a firefighter difficult. Equipment needs to be checked, dismantled and reassembled correctly, pressure gauges need to be read accurately, and when an emergency occurs you need to be on the ball mentally. Possessing common sense will help you get through the practical side of your training without endangering yourself or others.

LOGICAL THINKING

This is closely linked in with common sense. Logical thinkers are able to use the information they have been given and follow it through to its conclusion in a systematic way. They don't go off into

DID YOU KNOW?

After severe flooding at the 2005 Glastonbury Festival, Somerset FRS and a high volume pumping unit helped the show to go on by pumping approximately 3 million litres of flood water away from the area in a 12 hour operation.

Source: FRSonline (www.frsonline.gov.uk)

flights of fancy but think 'if I do A then B will follow which will lead me to C'. By following such thought processes they are able to make the correct decisions for each situation.

SITUATIONAL AWARENESS

When an emergency situation develops you will have many different things to think about all at once. What is the source of the fire; are there casualties; does the area need to be evacuated; what kind of equipment do you need; is there the possibility of the fire spreading and in what direction; could the weather conditions be a contributory factor? At times like these you have to be aware of every aspect of what is going on because by having situational awareness you can make the safest and most effective decisions. So, if you can think on your feet and keep mentally alert to all possibilities you'll make a more effective firefighter.

If you can think on your feet and keep mentally alert to all possibilities you'll make a more effective firefighter.

GOOD SELF-DISCIPLINE

It's a fact of life in the emergency services that you will be working a shift system. This will probably include nights, weekends and over some public holiday periods such as Christmas and Easter. If you can't be bothered with that and think you'd rather be out with your mates, or curled up in bed then you don't have the self-discipline for the job. You are also going to have to be disciplined about your fitness regime, about your drinking habits, about your personal appearance and your time-keeping habits. For example, time-keeping is so important to the emergency services that if you turn up a minute late for a job interview with the Manchester service you will be sent home without taking it.

ABILITY TO FOLLOW ORDERS

When people's lives are at stake you do not have the time to stand around arguing about who is going to do what. When the officer in command gives you an order, you carry it out to the best of your ability; it is as straightforward as that. You don't procrastinate, you don't leave it to other people, you just do it. If you have the ability to follow orders without fuss or bother it will make your progression through the service much easier.

When the officer in command gives you an order, you carry it out to the best of your ability.

Just as there are personal tools and strengths that will help you get on within the fire and emergency service, there are other personality traits and physical conditions that may make your passage less straightforward. As stated earlier, many of these are addressed during the training period, but knowing about them before you even apply may make it easier for you to decide whether this really is the career for you or not.

PHYSICAL DISABILITIES

Due to the Disabilities Discrimination Act 1995 the Fire and Rescue services must now assess each individual on his or her own physical abilities, but a good level of all-round physical fitness is needed to be a firefighter. However, if you suffer from any of the conditions below you may find a job more suited to your ability in another area of the fire and rescue services.

POOR EYESIGHT
As already stated you must have good eyesight without contact lenses or glasses. You should also have good colour vision, although Alex Dunnet notes 'if you do suffer from colour blindness we have to assess how bad it is before turning you down as a firefighter.'

VERTIGO (FEAR OF HEIGHTS)
Hampshire firefighter Rob Line says he knows quite a few firefighters who were initially scared of heights but have overcome their fear due to the training they received. However, if the thought of being on a stepladder makes you dizzy, or looking out from a tall building makes you sick to your stomach, you really need to ask yourself if a job that will frequently have you working at heights is really for you.

CLAUSTROPHOBIA (FEAR OF CONFINED SPACES)
The same is true if you hate working in small, cramped, confined spaces – especially if those spaces are dark and full of smoke. Once again, the exercises you have to do during your training should help you to control mild claustrophobia, but if you know such situations make you panic and bring you

DID YOU KNOW?

A new fire pump costs £150,000.

Source:
Get Firewise
(www.firekills.gov.uk)

out in a cold sweat you really need to reconsider if this is the career for you.

ASTHMA/OTHER RESPIRATORY DISORDERS

They say where there's smoke there's fire and the one thing you can count on if you are a firefighter is encountering a whole lot of smoke. If you suffer from asthma this could be a potentially life-threatening situation. Firefighters are issued with breathing apparatus but as Alex Dunnet explains 'the wind may change direction rapidly, the chemicals causing the smoke may be poisonous and sudden explosions can change the nature of the smoke you are inhaling and if you've got a face mask on and have an asthma attack you will not be able to use an inhaler.' Be realistic about just how bad your condition is because you want to be a help to other people, not a hindrance.

LACK OF DISCIPLINE

If your time-keeping is less than perfect and you can't keep yourself fit or your kit in order then you will not be pulling your weight within your watch. Remember, these people depend on you as much as you depend on them and if they can keep their self-discipline you owe it to them to keep yours.

DISLIKE OF AUTHORITY

If you really dislike taking orders and have a problem with authority figures you will not be able to cope with the hierarchical nature of the fire and emergency services. Someone has to be in charge and at the beginning of your career that certainly won't be you, so think long and hard about whether a job where you are more autonomous might be more suitable for you.

INABILITY TO DEAL WITH EMOTIONAL DISTRESS

It can be extremely distressing when you are called to emergencies where there are fatalities or serious injuries. There may be other family members or friends present who have survived who will need to be calmed down or comforted. If you don't possess the social skills to help in this kind of situation it can be personally distressing too. If you don't want to handle such emotional pain a job away from such interaction with the public may be more suitable.

SQUEAMISHNESS

If you are called to an enormous explosion or multiple pile-up on the motorway there's a fair chance you are going to see blood, gore, severed limbs and burned bodies. Some people take this in their stride, others find it makes them feel sick and faint. Be honest with yourself; are you the kind of person who turns away when they show real life operations on television? Or can you watch without any adverse reactions?

INTERVIEW QUESTIONS

Finally in this section here is a list of actual questions that have been asked of firefighting candidates at interview. Have a good old think about how you would answer them because they will give you a better idea of what the fire services are looking for.

- Do you have any experience of working in a team environment through social activities or jobs you have had?
- Have you any experiences of communicating with the general public? Can you communicate with a wide variety of different people? Give examples.

- Is keeping fit important to you? What sporting or exercise activities do you engage in?
- Have you ever been in a dangerous situation? What were your thoughts at the time?
- After attending a serious incident you are left to deal with a relative of someone who has been seriously injured. What would you do and say?
- How would you deal with the situation if someone on your watch was acting in a sexually or racially offensive manner?
- Once qualified and looking for promotion how would you feel about taking orders from someone younger than yourself?
- Have you worked with tools and equipment in the past? Talk about any practical experiences of manual work you have had.
- You are passing a building and there is a strong smell of gas, what would you do?
- Why should the fire services choose you over any of the other candidates here for interview?

DID YOU KNOW?

The 2004/2005 SEH (Survey of English Housing) estimates that 308,000 households in England experienced at least one domestic fire during the previous 12 months. Of the 308,000 households experiencing a fire, the SEH estimates about 273,000 households had a fire inside the house and in the remaining 35,000 households it was outside the house, eg in the garden.

Source: DCLG

4

A day with Blue Watch

The following is based on the experiences of firefighter Rob Line, who is a member of Blue Watch at High Town Fire Station, one of three full-time stations in Southampton, Hampshire. Hampshire operates the 2, 2, 4 shift system (two days on from 9am to 6pm, two nights on from 6pm to 9am, and four days off). There are 13 members of Blue Watch.

9AM TO 11AM: START WORK AT STATION

One of the first things a firefighter will be told is where he or she will be sitting in the fire engine if called out. They then check all the kit including their breathing apparatus. Over tea the watch will talk about any road closures in the area since the last shift that may affect getting to and from incidents. After this it is time for **routine** where they have a range of jobs to do including cleaning the fire station and appliances, such as the engines, and testing all the equipment. There is a set-down procedure for testing as some pieces of equipment must be tested daily, some weekly and some monthly.

11AM UNTIL LUNCH

The time from 11am until lunchtime is dedicated to training. Firefighters are constantly upgrading their skills with training and can be put forward for lots of courses. Once trained, they can then become instructors themselves, passing on their knowledge to other firefighters. Rob Line is a Physical

Training Instructor and also a Manual Handling Instructor. He has also taken and passed his LGV test (Light Goods Vehicle) in order to drive the fire engine and had to do a further course in order to be allowed to drive on blue lights (ie when the engine is answering an emergency call). Other training can involve ventilation, decontamination, trench rescues, first aid and safe access training.

Firefighters are constantly upgrading their skills with training and can be put forward for lots of courses. Once trained, they can then become instructors themselves, passing on their knowledge to other firefighters.

AFTER LUNCH UNTIL 4PM
The firefighters go out and do Community Fire Safety. This involves advising on fire safety and also fitting smoke alarms in private homes. Blue Watch is currently fitting fire alarms with special batteries that last ten years across the area. Hampshire has its own dedicated Schools Unit but if they are visiting a school and doing a display Blue Watch may be asked to take a fire engine out for the children to see first hand.

4PM TO 6PM
Return to station to get ready to hand over to the next watch.

At any time during the course of a shift Blue Watch may be called to an incident. High Town Fire Station gets approximately 2000 calls a year ranging from Special Service Calls (cats up trees or anything else that isn't a fire), to car accidents and assisting the ambulance, to children setting bins on fire. It also gets its fair share of hoax calls. Apparently, across England and Wales there are 135 hoax calls to the fire services a day and each hoax costs around £1700. Part of the work the Schools Unit does is to make children aware of the dangers of hoax calls (see 'Hoax fire calls' box below).

HOAX FIRE CALLS

The Fire and Rescue Service in England and Wales responds to about 50,000 hoax calls every year, or 135 per day. Each hoax costs £1700, which makes £230,000 a day or £84 million a year.

London Fire Brigade has the highest hoax call rate in the UK, attending nearly twice as many hoax call-outs (9686) as the second worst affected brigade, Greater Manchester (5268), and the West Midlands (4074).

If the fire services are called out under false pretences the danger is other calls, to real incidents, will have to wait, which could put lives at risk.

Making a hoax call is illegal, and the penalties for doing so are either a £5000 fine or six months in prison.

Source: DCLG

5

Making your mind up

Saving lives, preventing fires, cutting people from car wrecks and working with cutting-edge technology are just some of the things firefighters can expect to encounter during the course of their working lives, and because the fire services make us as a society feel safer and more protected, they are highly valued and admired. But how does being a firefighter affect the men and women who choose this as a career? What does it bring to their lives in terms of financial compensation, personal satisfaction and future prospects? In this chapter we look at some of the most frequently asked questions about joining the fire service and the answers here will help you to decide if this really is the career for you.

WHAT QUALIFICATIONS WILL I NEED?

For a start you have to be 18 years old or over. You will need at least five GCSEs grades A to C, and some brigades will ask for passes in specific subjects such as Mathematics, English and a science such as Physics or Chemistry. Many brigades will also ask for a clean driving license. You also need to be physically fit and to have good, unaided vision and not suffer from colour blindness. You will be checked to see if you have a criminal record – and don't even think about keeping a criminal record quiet because you will be found out! Even if you meet these criteria there is no guarantee you will get a training position because you have to go through the National Firefighter Selection Process

DID YOU KNOW?

London Fire Brigade is the top gay-friendly fire and rescue service in the UK according to campaigning organisation Stonewall. At 30th place on Stonewall's Workplace Equality Index, London Fire Brigade joins an elite group of organisations that includes blue chip FTSE 100 companies, government departments and local authorities. London Fire Brigade has proactively sought to increase firefighter recruitment from the gay and lesbian community by advertising campaigns and has held a recruitment open day targeted at the gay and lesbian community. In July of 2002 LFB held the first Pride Breakfast for fire service staff from all over the country. In 2004 this annual event was held at Soho fire station for staff of the brigade and business leaders from the gay community.

Source: London Fire Brigade

before being given a place on a training course. As stated before, competition is extremely fierce with up to 40 applicants for each place. In the 'Training Day' chapter you will find all you need to know about the initial selection process and subsequent training.

ONCE QUALIFIED, WILL I BE ABLE TO MOVE UP THE PROMOTION LADDER QUITE QUICKLY?

That will depend on your abilities and what you want out of the job. If you are ambitious and have a good level of skills after the initial two-year probation period you can move on quite quickly, especially now the Integrated Personal Development System (IPDS) has been introduced. Each individual is assessed and those deemed to have the highest potential are fast-tracked through the system so they can progress more quickly through the ranks. For example, if you are highly motivated and have good skills you can progress from firefighter through crew manager to watch manager in five years. By the time you are promoted to a managerial role such as station manager, you will have to undertake

specialist training at the Fire Service College based in
Moreton-in-Marsh in Gloucestershire (see 'The Fire Service
College' box on p 42). However, managerial roles mean the
work becomes less hands-on and more involved with
administration. This is why some firefighters such as Rob
Line of Hampshire FRS, who hates paperwork, prefer to
remain at the level of firefighter for the whole of their
careers. Promotions will normally be made internally within
your specific brigade up to the level of station manager.
From this level on vacancies are advertised across the fire
services, which means most senior officers will have
experience with a number of brigades.

WILL I BE ABLE TO TRAVEL WITH THE JOB?

Absolutely. From the above you can see that if you wish to
get on in the fire services you'll have to be willing to travel to
other brigades. Many brigades will accept transfers from
other brigades at the same level but you will have to serve a
minimum time with your original brigade before moving on.
In some instances, brigades charge what is known as a
'training bond' (ie the cost of the training you have received)
if you wish to move before a certain amount of time has
elapsed. This can add up to an eye-watering £10,000 so
check before you start your training.

Each individual is assessed and those deemed to
have the highest potential are fast-tracked
through the system so they can progress more
quickly through the ranks.

WILL I WORK A NINE-TO-FIVE DAY?

In most cases, no. The fire services work a shift system because the country needs fire cover 24/7 for 365 days of the year. Fires don't conveniently start only during office hours and many road accidents happen at night so control centres need to be manned and firefighters need to be on duty in order to cope with the emergencies (and while on-duty retained firefighters will be 'on call' at any time). The working week is 42 hours long and can include overtime. The shift pattern you work will depend on your particular brigade. Some work the 2, 2, 4 system described in the 'A Day with Blue Watch' chapter, others do five watches during the week. The average is to have two days off a week. Some people find shift work suits them very well; however it can be very disruptive to your sleep patterns and to your social life, so have a good think about how it would affect you if you were to join the fire service.

WOMAN FIREFIGHTERS INITIATIVE

On the 16th May 2006, the new Minister for the Fire and Rescue Service, Angela Smith, visited the London Fire Brigade training ground in Southwark to launch a new national advertising campaign, sponsored by the Department for Communities and Local Government, aimed at raising awareness among women of the possibilities of a frontline fire and rescue service career.

A significant reason for women being under-represented in operational roles in the fire and rescue service is because many see firefighting as a male occupation. The Minister urged would-be recruits not to be put off by this macho stereotype and the new campaign is designed to support the fire and rescue service in raising awareness of the benefits for women of a career as a firefighter and includes a national advertising campaign focused on high profile women's magazines. This activity is supported by posters, leaflets and postcards to be placed in health clubs, sports centres, cinemas and bars and pubs across England.

Angela Smith said: 'Firefighting is not a job open only to men. In a modern fire and rescue service we need recruits who are physically and mentally confident. Firefighting is a great career opportunity for those women who are fit and active and enjoy a challenge. This latest campaign forms part of a general drive towards greater equality and diversity in the fire and rescue service. The government remains committed to creating a modern workforce that genuinely reflects by age, disability, gender, race, religion and belief and sexuality, the community it serves. This will enable the service to connect with the harder to reach parts of our communities in order to save lives through fire prevention as well as through operational intervention.'

Visitors to the Department's website (www.communities. gov.uk) will be able to get free copies of the specially produced DVD *So You Want To Be A Firefighter?* which gives an insight into the day to day job of firefighters across the country.

Source: DCLG

WILL I GET TIME OFF FOR HOLIDAYS?

Of course you will. When you first join the service you get 28 days of holiday a year, alongside public holidays. If you are required to work on public holidays such as Christmas you are paid double time and will also receive time off in lieu. However, as there always has to be a certain amount of people on duty at any time you may find you can't always get time off when you want it. This is especially true over busy periods – people with families will want to have Christmas off and take their summer holidays to coincide with the school holidays.

HOW MUCH CAN I EXPECT TO EARN?

Pay rises as you become more experienced but all pay levels are good in the fire service. For example, as at 2005 a **trainee firefighter** would earn £19,394 per annum, and after the two-year probation period this would rise to £21,560, while an **experienced firefighter** could earn £25,850. A **crew manager** would start on £27,163 rising to £28,320, and a **watch manager** would start on £29,073 rising to £32,048. **Area managers** can earn upwards of £49,440.

Retained firefighters are paid an annual retainer of around £2020 for a **firefighter** rising to £3677 for a **station manager** and are also paid an hourly rate for any work they undertake which starts at around £9.22 for a **firefighter** rising to £16.79 for a **station manager**.

Control centre staff start on around £18,424 for a **trainee** while **group managers** can earn in excess of £40,433.

WHERE WILL I BE WORKING?

If you're a firefighter almost anywhere and everywhere!

Apart from doing your routine work such as checking and training at the fire station you will also be going into the community giving advice to nursing homes and other institutions on their fire prevention precautions, and checking local premises such as shops, hotels and clubs to make sure they conform to fire safety measures such as having adequate emergency exits that are not blocked, and having sufficient safety equipment such as fire blankets and extinguishers. You may also attend school open days with the fire engine in order to educate children about fire safety. Then there are the shouts you go on. You could be up a ladder attending a fire at a block of flats, attending a road accident where someone is trapped in their car, using special fire retardant foam at a chemical spill, pumping out flooded premises, or trying to get someone out of a stuck lift. Time and again firefighters say it is this variety and the fact they don't know what they will be doing from one day to the next that is the biggest attraction to the job. Control centre staff obviously won't be moving around in this way but their work too is very varied.

DID YOU KNOW?

Of the 13,400 accidental car fires in 2003/2004, 71% were due to vehicle defects, with defects in wiring and batteries being the biggest single cause. Only 8% of accidental car fires were caused by a crash or collision.

Source: DCLG

COULD I WORK AS A FIREFIGHTER OUTSIDE THE FIRE SERVICE?
There are certain places and organisations that have their own on-site fire services. These include Army military bases, the Royal Naval Dockyards, Royal Air Force bases and the British Airports Authority (BAA). You will need to

contact BAA and the Defence Fire Service direct to find out about recruitment, training and job specifications (see the 'Resources' chapter).

WHAT CAN I EXPECT TO GET OUT OF THE INDUSTRY, PERSONALLY?

A great deal of satisfaction that you are really making a difference to your community. Preventing fires and rescuing people from burning buildings and from wrecked cars is an incredibly worthwhile thing to do for a living. In some instances you can take great pride from the fact someone has lived because of your intervention. Even what seem like mundane tasks such as fitting fire alarms can really make a difference to the safety of your community. Apart from that you'll be doing a job that is interesting with a bunch of people who are not only your workmates but who could possibly be your best friends too. These are the men and women who watch your back as you watch theirs and it is not unusual for fellow firefighters to form lifelong friendships. Finally, think of the achievement you will feel as you return to the station at the end of your watch with yet another fire put out or another person saved.

These are the men and women who watch your back as you watch theirs and it is not unusual for fellow firefighters to form lifelong friendships.

HOW WILL THE WIDER PUBLIC VIEW ME?

With both respect and gratitude. Just the sight of a fire engine racing along to an emergency can be incredibly reassuring to members of the public because it shows them if they were ever in need the fire services would be there for them too. Like police officers, firefighters are held in great respect by the wider community. However, as is always the case, there are some people who do not share that respect. Attacks on firefighters are now at an all time high with 393 attacks being logged in a ten month period in 2005 (source: Sky News). Most of these consisted of children throwing stones at fire engines and it is hoped that with more education the attacks can be stopped. In Oldham Project Firefly has been set up to bring teenagers into stations to see what firefighters do first hand and since Firefly began attacks have dropped in Oldham by 55%. However, it must be emphasised that this is definitely minority behaviour and the vast majority of people are pleased and grateful for the protection the fire service provides.

WHAT CAN I START DOING NOW TO GIVE ME A BETTER CHANCE OF SUCCEEDING IN THE FIRE SERVICES?

Make sure you get the grades you need in key subjects such as English and Mathematics. Find out if it is possible to take a BTEC National Diploma in Public Services at a local college, which will show

DID YOU KNOW?

Road vehicle fires totalled 72,800 in 2004, of which 60,300 (83%) were in cars, 4800 (7%) were in vans and 2000 (3%) were in lorries. The total number of fires recorded in road vehicles decreased by 22% (20,000 less fires) compared with 2003 and follows an 8% fall between 2002 and 2003. This is the third consecutive reduction in road vehicle fires following successive increases between 1997 and 2001. Those increases were mainly due to rises in deliberate car fires.

Source: DCLG

you really have a desire and interest in the wider community. Also, start doing some form of physical exercise – you may well be asked at interview if you belong to a sports team or fitness club. If there's a fire station near you pop in and talk to some of the staff. Firefighter Rob Line says stations are friendly places and the firefighters will be more than happy to talk to you. Find out the web address of your local brigade (see the 'Resources' chapter) because you will find information there on any open days they may be having (called 'have a go' days) or if they operate work placements. Also see if they operate a Junior Firefighter scheme. You can become a Junior Firefighter from 16 years of age.

THE FIRE SERVICE COLLEGE

The Fire Service College at Moreton-in-Marsh has been operational for 38 years. Up to 600 students can stay on the site and it has its own self-contained leisure centre with squash courts, a swimming pool, a fitness room and a large, multi-sports hall. Outdoors there are football and rugby pitches and a golf practice area.

It offers professionally validated courses in fire safety and fire engineering from foundation to degree level. Many of its tutors are seconded from United Kingdom fire brigades and are experienced in the practical application of the latest fire safety legislation and technology. They are supported by specialist chemists, engineers, building tutors and fire engineers.

It has a large training ground where incident scenarios are simulated such as building fires and accidents, while road, rail, aircraft and shipping incidents, and chemical plant, oil storage, industrial and offshore emergencies are created routinely.

Source: Fire Service College
(www.fireservicecollege.ac.uk)

JIM GILL

Case study 2

6

CREW MANAGER, RETAINED DUTY SYSTEM (RDS)

Forty-two-year-old Jim is a self-employed domestic appliance service engineer who first became interested in the fire service back in 1990. However, as he had just started his own business he did not have enough spare time to make the huge commitment joining the retained system requires. In 1998, with his business now well established and looking for a new challenge, he applied and duly went through the training system before becoming a retained firefighter at Thornbury in South Gloucestershire. Jim has recently been promoted to crew manager, which qualifies him to take a pump out in charge. He has his LGV (Light Goods Vehicle) license and so can drive the fire engine and he recently attended his first Retained Junior Officer (RJO) course at the Fire Service College at Moreton-in-Marsh in Gloucestershire.

'I have the same duties as a wholetime firefighter and I am trained to deal with road traffic accidents (RTA), house fires, car fires, cats up trees and cows in slurry pits. As a crew manager I have specific jobs to do

Joining the retained service is a life-changing event.

like ordering equipment and stationery and making sure we have enough firefighters available (at present we are a bit short on manpower). There's also shed loads of paperwork.

'What I enjoy most about the job is the camaraderie. We do fall out from time to time but when we are working together we all pull together. It's being part of a team. I also love the moment when my alerter goes off (but not at 2am in the morning) because I never know what I might be going to. Quite often it's just an alarm going off but the other morning we were called to a car fire in Thornbury High Street with a person trapped inside. When we arrived the car was well alight with what remained of a man and his dog still in the vehicle. After we had put the car out we discovered the man had committed suicide by emptying a can of petrol onto his lap and setting fire to it. However, such occurrences are rare in sleepy Thornbury.

'The downside to the job I now do is having to account for every action for statistical purposes, which is very time consuming and it does interrupt my working day and if I let it, it could rule my life. Joining the retained service is a life-changing event. You must commit yourself to be available X amount of the day and week. It will interrupt your work, meals, sleep, sport and social time, also committing yourself to abstaining from alcohol for a weekend can be a bit much for some young people. One retired firefighter told me he missed out on his children growing up because he didn't want to miss the next shout. I've tried hard to make sure that hasn't happened to me.

'I think to be a good firefighter you need to be fit and you need to be practical. You also need to be able to do what you are told but also able to make your own decisions. You must be a team player and be able to absorb information quickly and under stress, but I'd also like to add that it's not rocket science!

'To me the commitment I give is worth it. The job is the best in the world and the money is not bad. I would like to be promoted again, if the opportunity arises. The highest rank I can achieve is the next one up, known as watch manager. What I want to do is gain as much experience and qualifications as I can to use both within and outside the service. Ultimately, when I retire from the service I hope I can say that I enjoyed the whole of my career and that it was fun.'

BUNCEFIELD OIL DEPOT BLAZE

On Sunday 11th December 2005, the largest ever fire to be seen in peacetime UK and Europe erupted at the **Buncefield oil depot**, Leverstock Green, near Hemel Hempstead. The fire destroyed as much as £200 million worth of fuel being held at the depot, while 2000 people in the area were evacuated and there were 43 casualties.

About 600 firefighters from across the country were called in to tackle the blaze using a mixture of flame retardant foam mixed with water. About 250,000 litres of foam mixed with 32,000 litres of water per minute were pumped into the flames. In all more than 15 million litres of water and 250,000 litres of foam concentrate were used and requests for more foam were sent out across the country while water was brought in from the Grand Union Canal using high-pressure hoses. After being used on the blaze the foam/water mix was held in a specially created man-made lake before being transferred to tankers and taken to centres where it was processed and made safe.

In all, there were 20 fires at the site, which created a huge black cloud of smoke primarily made up of hydrocarbons. This caused a major pollution alert with nearby Haringey experiencing a spike in pollution at 6pm on the Sunday evening and people were advised to stay inside with their windows closed.

The fire was started when inflammable petrol vapour seeped from a storage tank and was ignited, probably due to an electrical fault.

Source: *Evening Standard*

Training day

7

By its very nature, the job of firefighter is potentially far more dangerous than sitting in an office working the 9 to 5. However the truth is that due to the rigorous training firefighters have to undergo there are thankfully few fatalities within the modern-day fire services. In fact, in 2004, there were 508 fire-related deaths in the UK, and only three of these fatalities were firefighters (in 2003 there was only one). Obviously, the fire services would prefer there to be none at all and to this end firefighter training is being constantly refined and upgraded. But before you even get to the training stage, you have to get through the National Firefighter Selection process. This initial process makes sure only those candidates who really have what it takes proceed to the training stage. This is because firefighter training is an intense and costly business (as stated before some brigades charge what is known as a 'training bond' (ie the cost of the training you have received) if you wish to move to another brigade before a certain amount of time has elapsed after your training. This can be as much as £10,000) and the fire service would prefer to take its time picking only those candidates who have a good chance of successfully completing the course rather than wasting money on those who will not.

NATIONAL FIREFIGHTER SELECTION
On the following page you will find a quick reference chart mapping the selection process. Take a look at it before reading in more detail what actually happens.

SELECTION PROCESS FOR PROSPECTIVE FIREFIGHTERS

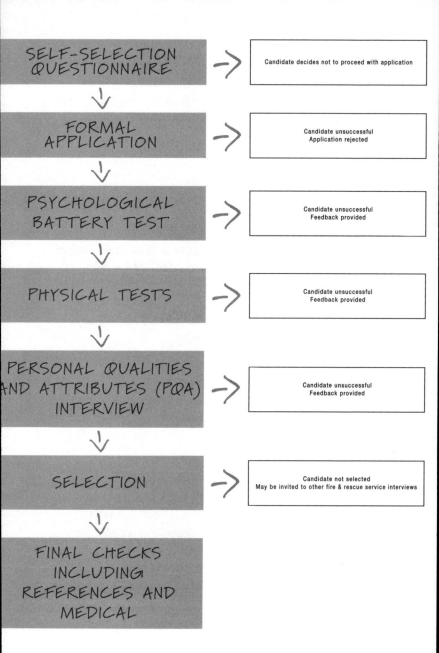

SELF-SELECTION QUESTIONNAIRE → Candidate decides not to proceed with application

FORMAL APPLICATION → Candidate unsuccessful Application rejected

PSYCHOLOGICAL BATTERY TEST → Candidate unsuccessful Feedback provided

PHYSICAL TESTS → Candidate unsuccessful Feedback provided

PERSONAL QUALITIES AND ATTRIBUTES (PQA) INTERVIEW → Candidate unsuccessful Feedback provided

SELECTION → Candidate not selected May be invited to other fire & rescue service interviews

FINAL CHECKS INCLUDING REFERENCES AND MEDICAL

WHO IS ELIGIBLE?

To become a firefighter you must be 18 years or over and most services will ask for at least five GCSE passes at grades A–C (or S level, grades 2–3). Some services specify you have GCSEs in Mathematics, English and science subjects.

HOW DO I APPLY?

Most fire services now have information on their recruitment practises (and if they are actually recruiting) on their websites (see 'Resources' chapter). Some services also recruit by placing adverts on TV, in newspapers and on radio. Before you formally apply you can ask for a copy of the self-selection questionnaire (SSQ). This consists of some basic questions that will give you a good idea whether you are a suitable candidate or not. If you still believe firefighting is for you now is the time to formally apply.

WHAT HAPPENS NEXT?

If your application is approved you will be invited to undergo a point of entry selection test which normally consists of at least two days of testing.

DAY ONE

This consists of a criminal record check and a battery of psychometric tests to ascertain if you have the mental abilities to handle the job. At this stage you will also have to undergo a blood pressure test and an auditory test. If you are unsuccessful at this stage you will be given feedback on why this is so. If you are successful you will be invited back to day two.

DAY TWO

Now your physical abilities will be tested. The following are standard National Occupational tests, which all firefighters must pass.

- **The Dead Lift Test.** You must raise 50 kg to a standing position in five seconds and hold it there for five seconds before lowering it.
- **The Ladder Extension Test.** You must raise the extending part of a ladder weighing 60 kg to the top of the extending line within 20 seconds and then lower it under control.
- **The Ladder Climb Test.** This test will check whether you suffer from vertigo (fear of heights) or not. You must climb a 13.5 m ladder to third floor height and take the 'leg lock' position (with the inside of your knee hooked around one of the rungs) while you let go of the ladder and answer some basic questions.
- **The Confined Space Test.** This test will check whether you suffer from claustrophobia. You must enter a cage system in total darkness while wearing breathing apparatus and negotiate a crawl way within three minutes. You will be given spoken directions.
- **The Hose Run Test.** You must run out with a 70 mm delivery hose and make up five lengths within six minutes.

Other tests you may be given include dismantling and reassembling a piece of

DID YOU KNOW?

A firefighter is fit enough to:

- Run two miles in under 20 minutes
- Swim 600 metres in under 20 minutes
- Cycle 8 miles in less than 33 minutes

Source: Get Firewise (www.firekills.gov.uk)

equipment by using written instructions. If you manage to get this far, well done! None of these tests is easy. However, if you are unsuccessful, feedback will be given on where you have gone wrong. Those who do pass these tests will be invited back to undergo a Personal Qualities and Attributes (PQAs) Interview that lasts approximately 30 minutes. This tests the seven areas or 'scales' of ability most important to becoming a competent modern firefighter. These are:

1. Working with others
2. Commitment to diversity and integrity
3. Confidence and resilience
4. Commitment to excellence
5. Commitment to development
6. Situational awareness
7. Openness to change.

Before you start panicking, you do not need any prior knowledge of the fire services in order to answer these questions and a practise booklet should be made available to you prior to attending the PQA Interview so you can familiarise yourself with the style of the questions, most of which are multiple choice. Again, if you fail at this stage, feedback will be provided. However, if you are successful you will then only need to pass a full medical and to have your references checked before being offered a place on a training programme.

A practise booklet should be made available to you prior to attending the PQA Interview so you can familiarise yourself with the style of the questions, most of which are multiple choice.

FIREFIGHTER TRAINING

As stated before, firefighter training is constantly being improved and new schemes will be implemented throughout 2006/2007 and so the following is only an approximation of what may happen during the training period. Also, the training will vary from fire service to fire service so you need to check with the particular service you are interested in joining.

After successfully completing the National Firefighters Selection process you are issued with an enrolment pack giving information on the training course. The initial training period – induction or Phase 1 – usually lasts for approximately 14/16 weeks, can be residential or non-residential, and takes place at your particular services training centre. The training consists of a mix of practical exercises, role-play, group discussion, simulations and demonstrations, and written work and at the end of each week, or when a unit of work is completed, you must produce a summary (usually consisting of multiple choice questions and written answers) of what you have learned. The summaries are then assessed to see how you are progressing and if you need more help you will receive more concentrated tutoring. Trainees have

DID YOU KNOW?

Britain's all-time favourite TV advert was recently voted to be the 1973 Hovis ad where 13-year-old Carl Barlow wearing a cloth cap was seen pushing his bike up a very steep hill. Thirty-three years on Carl is now a firefighter based at Islington Fire Station in London. 'My time as the Hovis boy was fun,' he says 'but as a career I'll stick to putting out fires.'

Source:
Evening Standard

full access to their tutors at all times during the course and can go to them for advice and support on any matter. They also have full access to the internet so they can view firefighter development e-learning modules.

With the introduction of the new IPDS (Integrated Personal Development System) every probationer will be given the chance to progress either upwards through the ranks or to further develop their skills depending on their ability.

The course is broken down into separate units that cover all aspects of a firefighter's work. These include:

- Using your PPE (protective personal equipment) including the breathing apparatus
- Basic rescue techniques and learning about the way fire behaves
- The use of equipment such as ladders, knots, hoses and hydraulic equipment
- The use of foam and other chemical fire retardants/extinguishers
- How to enter a smoke-filled room
- Health, safety and risk management
- How to treat casualties, administer first aid and support people at incidents
- Giving fire safety advice in the community
- Environmental and structural risks of buildings and other structures

- Dealing with transport incidents
- Dealing with HAZMAT (hazardous materials)
- Personal development
- Equal opportunities and discrimination legislation.

Below is an illustration of what a typical week's training might look like.

	MORNING	**AFTERNOON**
MONDAY	Parade/Key skills	Working near water/ Fire awareness
TUESDAY	Physical training/ Pumps and ladders	Pumps and ladders
WEDNESDAY	Parade with watch	Safe access training
THURSDAY	Physical training/ Pump drills	Ladder drills
FRIDAY	Parade/Written assessment	Ladders assessment (weekly)/Pump assessment (weekly)

Source: Kent Fire and Rescue Service

At the end of the course there is a Passing Out Parade and the trainees must then complete a further two-year probationary period at their home fire station before becoming fully qualified firefighters. During this period – Phase 2 – they continue to learn on the job with the more experienced firefighters at the station acting as tutors. Again, progress is assessed and this training leads to vocational qualifications such as Emergency Fire Services Operations in the Community NVQ levels 2 and 3. Other professional qualifications can be gained at the specialist Fire Service College at Moreton-in-Marsh where fire engineering can be studied from foundation to degree level. With the introduction of the new IPDS (Integrated Personal Development System) every probationer will be given the chance to progress either upwards through the ranks or to further develop their skills depending on their ability. The most talented individuals can be fast-tracked through the system, allowing them to achieve their full potential, which could lead all the way up through the seven vocational levels (firefighter, crew manager, watch manager, station manager, group manager, area manager, brigade manager). However, those who like the variety and hands-on nature of the work in the role of firefighter can undertake further training and branch sideways into other roles such as fire service trainer (see 'Case Study 1' with Rob Line).

access to

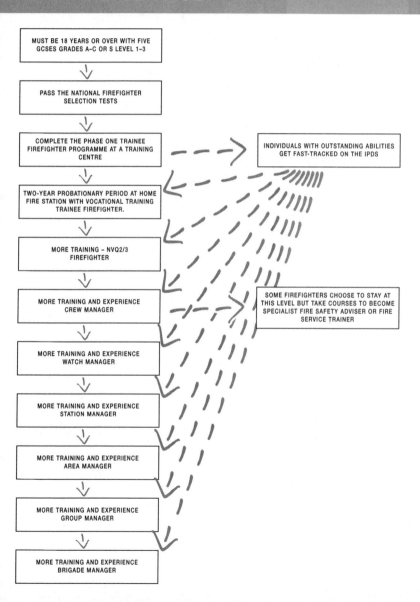

MUST BE 18 YEARS OR OVER WITH FIVE GCSES GRADES A–C OR S LEVEL 1–3

PASS THE NATIONAL FIREFIGHTER SELECTION TESTS

COMPLETE THE PHASE ONE TRAINEE FIREFIGHTER PROGRAMME AT A TRAINING CENTRE

INDIVIDUALS WITH OUTSTANDING ABILITIES GET FAST-TRACKED ON THE IPDS

TWO-YEAR PROBATIONARY PERIOD AT HOME FIRE STATION WITH VOCATIONAL TRAINING TRAINEE FIREFIGHTER.

MORE TRAINING – NVQ2/3 FIREFIGHTER

MORE TRAINING AND EXPERIENCE CREW MANAGER

SOME FIREFIGHTERS CHOOSE TO STAY AT THIS LEVEL BUT TAKE COURSES TO BECOME SPECIALIST FIRE SAFETY ADVISER OR FIRE SERVICE TRAINER

MORE TRAINING AND EXPERIENCE WATCH MANAGER

MORE TRAINING AND EXPERIENCE STATION MANAGER

MORE TRAINING AND EXPERIENCE AREA MANAGER

MORE TRAINING AND EXPERIENCE GROUP MANAGER

MORE TRAINING AND EXPERIENCE BRIGADE MANAGER

8

CARLY TAYLOR

Case study 3

ROOKIE FIREFIGHTER

Twenty-five-year-old Carly Taylor never intended to be a firefighter, she actually wanted to be a paramedic. However, when she was 17, a friend's partner who was in the retained service at Edenbridge in Kent told her they were desperate for more volunteers. At the time she was too young, but when she became 18 she joined the retained service and realised firefighting was what she wanted to do with her life. She stayed in the retained service for five years while working in the fitness industry and gaining qualifications as a lifeguard, a gym instructor, an ASA Swimming Teacher and in Speedo Aquafit. When she was 22 she applied to join the London Fire Service and was accepted. She started her training at Southwark in London in February 2005 and passed out five months later in June. Since then she has been working from the Whitechapel Station and just one month after she started, on the 7th July 2005, she was part of the first fire crew to attend the Aldgate bomb blast, giving first aid to those who had been injured.

'Whitechapel is a good area to work in because it is a mix of low income housing

Don't be put off by stereotypical views. I want people to judge me on how good I am as a firefighter rather than because I'm female doing the job.

and the City (of London) so there's a lot of variety in what I do. I've already had shouts to a few flat fires, to people locked inside their flats, road traffic accidents and lots and lots of people stuck in lifts! The only animal rescue I've done was a cat on a balcony. We've also gone out on an awful lot of false alarms. Obviously the bombings were the biggest thing I have ever been involved in during the course of my career, but at the time it didn't really sink in what I was dealing with. The call-out had just told us there had been an explosion in the street behind Aldgate tube station and so we only had two machines (fire engines) there with eight crew and I didn't have time to think about what I was doing or what had happened because it was so busy. The full impact of it only came home when I was watching it on TV later; that hit me harder than actually being there and it was difficult to get my head around.

'What I love about this job is working with the people on my crew – I love the whole support thing – and I also like never knowing what I will be facing from day to day because you never know what you are going to get called out to next. It's hard graft and it really challenges you and that's great – if there's something you don't think you can achieve in this job then just keep working at it and facing that challenge. The downside is seeing people going through awful things like the bombing, seeing the destruction and suffering it causes people. But doing this job is worthwhile because you are helping people who are in need and being able to help gives you plenty of satisfaction. It's good to know you are making a difference to someone individually and to society. I know I made a difference after the bombings and I get a real sense of achievement from that.

DID YOU KNOW?

London Fire Brigade have four specialist dogs (three Labradors named Jet, Sam and Sapphire and an English Springer Spaniel named Roscoe) who are trained to detect whether accelerants such as petrol have been used in suspected arson cases. In a 10m x 10m square test on carpet, a trained fire investigation dog will detect the presence of an accelerant in around two minutes or less. A fire investigator using specialist equipment will take on average two hours. The dogs wear special fire wellies to protect their paws.

Source: London Fire Brigade (www.london-fire.gov.uk)

'In this job you have to be open to change, every day is different, it is not structured like a 9 to 5. You also have to be willing and happy to be part of a team because you will always be relying on other people to help you. I say, just be open to the adventure of it all! If you are seriously considering joining the fire service then do your research on the job. It's not all what you see on TV and so find out if there are any open days you can attend to see what it is really like.

'I can see myself in the fire service for the rest of my working life; this is where I want to be until I retire. In fact, I like it so much I've applied to go back doing retained firefighting on my days off! I'd like to stay as a firefighter at the moment, although I would consider progressing to crew manager. However, I don't want to progress too far up the promotional ladder because then you get less hands-on and you're telling people what to do rather than being really physical. The fire service is perceived as a male dominated job but don't be put off by stereotypical views. I want people to judge me on how good I am as a firefighter rather than because I'm a female doing the job.'

THE FORENSIC FIRE SERVICE
BY GEMMA GREEN, FORENSIC SCIENCE SERVICE LTD

What does a forensic fire investigator actually do?
We investigate the origin and cause of fires (where, how and when the fire started) by visiting scenes of fires, normally at the request of the police, and recovering and examining the evidence that is left. We will also examine items recovered from fire scenes in the laboratory. Most of our lab work is to identify the presence of flammable liquids on debris taken from scenes but we also inspect and test appliances, carry out burning tests, examine clothing for flashburns and look at incendiary (but not explosive) devices.

How do you become a forensic fire investigator (FFI)? Do you train to become a forensic scientist and then specialise?
In the Forensic Science Service (FSS) we recruit internally, taking a person who is usually a casework-reporting officer and then training them in fire investigation. The training process is similar in many ways to an apprenticeship, taking 18 months to two years to complete. The trainee will start reporting laboratory examinations after about a year. At the end of two years the trainee should be capable of dealing with virtually any fire scene that they are asked to attend. It's true to say though that the process never stops, after a time training tails off and professional development comes to the fore.

Do FFIs work both at scenes of fires and in laboratories?

Yes. In our case the patterns of demand mean that we spend about half our time on scene investigations and the rest in the laboratory on analysis and testing.

Is there a specific job promotion route?

Not specifically for fire investigators, generally in the FSS an individual's role description will define their grade. Staff will receive a promotion when they start reporting their own cases, however scene work is at the top end of a forensic scientist's responsibilities and will eventually result in further promotion.

How long does training take and what qualifications do you need to apply?

FSS policy is that reporting officers must have degrees, but apart from this we find that attitude, enthusiasm, good people skills, broad scientific knowledge and flexibility are more important than the type of degree. The nature of the work we do favours a 'hard' science background such as chemistry, physics or engineering but any reasonably numerate biologist or toxicologist could become a successful fire investigator. (See www.forensic.gov.uk)

Career opportunities

9

From this guide you'll have seen that working within the fire services offers tremendous opportunities for advancement. Up to the rank of station commander promotion usually takes place from within each individual brigade, but vacancies for area manager, group manager and brigade manager are advertised throughout the service, so there is also the opportunity to travel and work around the country. Officers can also attend management and command training courses to gain the man management and administrative skills they need. They are also taught communication skills as they may have to work with representatives from local authorities and central government departments and to negotiate with fire service unions – some may even get to appear on television.

Most firefighters view what they do as a 'job for life' and would not dream of leaving the fire service, staying right up to retirement. However, those who do leave have skills and abilities that ensure they can easily move into other occupations such as fire marshal, ambulance person, coastguard officer, security officer or the armed forces.

In 2003/2004 the main cause of domestic fire was accidents whilst cooking (53%):

- Most domestic fires were started in the kitchen (60%)
- The majority of fires were discovered between 6pm and midnight (43%)
- Most domestic fires were discovered because the person was in the room when it started (30%)
- The fire and rescue service were called to 22% of domestic fires
- The vast majority of fires resulted in no personal injury (91%)
- 10% of households in England do not own any fire safety measures
- 80% of households own a working smoke alarm, with a further 6% owning a non-working alarm.

Source: DCLG

However, many firefighters love what they do so much they make the decision to stay in that role for the whole of their working lives. This doesn't mean they stop learning though as they can keep taking courses to add to their knowledge. Some take courses to become trainers in particular aspects of firefighting, such as Breathing Apparatus Instruction, thus passing on what they know to the next generation of firefighters. Others take courses that will give them specialised skills for working in particular areas. For instance at Kent Fire and Emergency Services not only do they deal with routine fires but they are also responsible for fire and safety at the Channel Tunnel, Dungeness nuclear power station, cliff rescues (they have line rescue teams at Deal and Folkestone) and they have a team of 90 firefighters and officers on standby to go to ship fires via helicopter. In March 2006 a new rapid reaction unit called the Maritime Incidents Response Group was set up to deal with major emergencies at sea.

Another specialist area is working for a Schools Unit, travelling around the schools in your county teaching children all about fire safety. As you can see, even if you decide not to work your way up through the ranks there are many opportunities to

THE MARITIME INCIDENTS RESPONSE GROUP

On the morning of Saturday 6th May 2006, there was an engine room fire onboard the cruise ship *Calypso*. Hampshire Fire and Rescue Service (HFRS) sent a liaison officer to the Coastguard office at Lee-on-Solent and two specialist officers to the casualty ship to assist with its safe journey into Southampton. The two HFRS officers, both members of the Maritime Incident Response Group (MIRG) boarded the *Calypso* to liaise with colleagues from East Sussex Fire and Rescue Service and to assess the additional HFRS resources required.

The fire broke out in the starboard engine room in the early hours of Saturday morning whilst the ship was approximately 20 miles off the coast of Eastbourne. Fire and Rescue MIRG teams in Hampshire, East Sussex and Kent were alerted to the incident. At around 4am, 18 members of the East Sussex team were airlifted to the scene. Hampshire and Kent teams remained on standby. The fire was contained to the engine room by the ship's carbon dioxide fire extinguishing system and a firefighting hose operated by two members of the ship's crew. All 700 passengers and crew were put on full emergency alert and were standing-by to abandon the ship. However, the situation was quickly assessed and a full evacuation was not carried out. Due to the fire damage and subsequent loss of power the ship was towed into Southampton to allow passengers to disembark and to enable fire crews to fully inspect the engine room to ensure the fire was fully extinguished.

The ship arrived safely in Southampton docks where an officer, two fire and rescue crews from St Mary's and Redbridge Hill fire stations and an Aerial Ladder Platform relieved the onboard emergency crews to assess the situation and assist with disembarkation. HFRS crews remained in attendance until just before 11pm when responsibility was handed back to the ship's crew.

Source: www.hantsfire.gov.uk

expand your knowledge and skill set. Most firefighters view what they do as a 'job for life' and would not dream of leaving the fire service, staying right up to retirement. However, those who do leave have skills and abilities that ensure they can easily move into other occupations such as fire marshal, ambulance person, coastguard officer, security officer or the armed forces.

The last word

By now, you should have a good idea of whether a role within the fire services is really what you want to do as a career and if you do then you are in good company – there are always far more applicants for jobs in this area than actual places available. Even though you can't apply to join until you are 18 there are already lots of things you could be doing to increase your chances of being one of the successful candidates.

GET FIT!

Firefighters have to be fit to do their jobs so join a gym or an exercise class, go swimming, or apply to get on your school football/rugby/hockey/netball team.

ATTEND AN OPEN DAY OR 'HAVE A GO' DAY

Many fire brigades across the country now have open days or 'have a go' days where you are shown around a station and actual firefighters explain what they do and may even demonstrate how some of the equipment works. You can find out if your local brigade is having any such events by looking at their website (see 'Resources' chapter).

JOIN THE CADETS (JUNIOR FIREFIGHTER SCHEME)

Some brigades have cadet units or a Junior Firefighter Scheme that you can join from the age of 16. Although these concentrate on fire safety and awareness they will still give you a good idea about whether this is the career for you or not. Once again check with your local brigade's website.

Becoming a firefighter is a serious undertaking and if the only reason you want to do this job is for the perceived glamour then forget it, you won't even get through the selection process.

JOIN THE RETAINED FIREFIGHTERS

If you are older and unemployed or already in another job, but think you'd like to have a go then you can join the retained system (see 'Case Study 2' with Jim Gill) from the age of 18. There is usually a shortage of retained firefighters around the country so your joining would be much appreciated. At any time, there are probably as many retained members of the fire and rescue service on duty as wholetime firefighters, and RDS personnel provide emergency cover to more than 60% of the UK. They play a vital role, especially in rural areas and have strong ties with their local communities. Once again, contact your local brigade for more information.

KEEP UP YOUR SCHOOL GRADES

Remember, there are far more applicants than places available so give yourself a better chance of being successful by getting good grades, especially in English and Mathematics. Taking a science-based subject such as Physics or Chemistry is also a good idea. If your local college offers it then take a BTEC National Diploma in Public Services.

DO A FIRST AID COURSE

You will be taught first aid if you get in to the fire service but it's good to show you are already interested in the subject.

TAKE AN INTEREST IN YOUR LOCAL COMMUNITY

If possible, try to undertake some voluntary work in your local community as this will show you are community spirited.

Becoming a firefighter is a serious undertaking and if the only reason you want to do this job is for the perceived glamour then forget it, you won't even get through the selection process. However, if you want to help individuals by reducing the risk of injury, damage or even death during fires and emergencies, and if you want to educate your local community by giving talks and demonstrations on fire safety, this is the job for you. However, before contacting your local brigade, take a look at the quick checklist below to see if you've really got what it takes to make a career in the fire services.

THE LAST WORD

DO YOU LIKE BEING PHYSICAL?

☐ YES
☐ NO

DO YOU LIKE WORKING WITH PEOPLE?

☐ YES
☐ NO

CAN YOU THINK CLEARLY UNDER PRESSURE?

☐ YES
☐ NO

ARE YOU PREPARED TO WORK SHIFTS?

☐ YES
☐ NO

CAN YOU COMMUNICATE EFFECTIVELY WITH
LOTS OF DIFFERENT PEOPLE?

☐ YES
☐ NO

DO YOU TAKE AN ACTIVE INTEREST IN YOUR
LOCAL COMMUNITY?

☐ YES
☐ NO

DO YOU LIKE WORK WITH A LOT OF VARIETY?

☐ YES
☐ NO

ARE YOU A SELF-STARTER, ABLE TO TAKE
CONTROL AND RESPONSIBILITY?

☐ YES
☐ NO

If you answered 'YES' to all these questions then
CONGRATULATIONS! YOU'VE CHOSEN THE RIGHT CAREER
If you answered 'NO' to any of these questions then a career as a firefighter may not be
for you, however there are still plenty of other jobs within the fire service that may suit
your talents better such as IT specialist, fire control operator, or admin or secretarial staff

Resources

GENERAL

UK FIRE SERVICE RESOURCES
This comprehensive website is run by a firefighter and includes sections on firefighters' pay, the history of the fire service and even job vacancies.
www.fireservice.co.uk

CONNEXIONS
This excellent website has details on a vast array of jobs including those in the fire service. Click onto the jobs4u Careers database.
www.connexions-direct.com

DEPARTMENT OF COMMUNITIES AND LOCAL GOVERNMENT
The government department responsible for the fire service. The website gives details of government policies and targets, fire safety and information on how services are being equipped and prepared for major emergencies.
www.communities.gov.uk

FORENSIC FIRE SERVICE
The Forensic Fire Service is part of the Forensic Science Service.
www.forensic.gov.uk

FRS ONLINE
A government website giving information about the fire and rescue services including employment, pay, hours, etc.
www.frsonline.fire.gov.uk

THE INSTITUTE OF FIRE ENGINEERS
London Road
Moreton-in-Marsh
Gloucestershire
GL56 0RH
Tel. 01608 812580
www.ife.org.uk

RETAINED FIREFIGHTERS' UNION (RFU)
Firefighter House
Station Road
Attleborough
Norfolk
NR17 2AS
Tel. 01953 455005
www.rfuonline.co.uk

FIRE SERVICE COLLEGE
London Road
Moreton-in-Marsh
Gloucestershire
GL56 0RH
www.fireservicecollege.ac.uk

SEPARATE FIRE SERVICES

BRITISH AIRPORTS AUTHORITY (BAA)
The BAA has its own fire services at Britain's airports. Go
into the website and click onto careers to find out about
vacancies.
www.baa.com

DEFENCE FIRE SERVICE

The Ministry of Defence (MOD) is responsible for the Defence Fire Service covering military, RAF and Royal Naval sites. Go into the site and click onto the jobseekers section for more information.

www.mod.uk

UK FIRE SERVICES

AVON FIRE BRIGADE

Temple Back
Bristol
BS1 6EU
Tel. 0117 926 2061
www.avonfire.gov.uk

BEDFORDSHIRE AND LUTON FIRE AND RESCUE SERVICE

Southfields Road
Kempston
Bedford
MK42 7NR
Tel. 01234 351081
www.bedsfire.com

BUCKINGHAMSHIRE FIRE AND RESCUE SERVICE

Brigade Headquarters
Stocklake
Aylesbury
Buckinghamshire
HP20 1BD
Tel. 01296 424666
www.bucksfire.gov.uk

CAMBRIDGESHIRE FIRE AND RESCUE SERVICE
Hinchingbrooke Cottage
Brampton Road
Huntingdon
PE29 2NA
Tel. 01480 444500
www.cambsfire.gov.uk

CENTRAL SCOTLAND FIRE BRIGADE
Main Street
Maddiston
Falkirk
FK2 0LG
Tel. 01324 716996
www.centralscotlandfire.gov.uk

CHESHIRE FIRE BRIGADE
Fire Brigade Headquarters
Winsford
Cheshire
CW7 2FQ
Tel. 01606 868700
www.cheshirefire.co.uk

CLEVELAND FIRE BRIGADE
Endeavour House
Stockton Road
Hartlepool
Cleveland
TS25 5TB
Tel. 01429 872311
www.clevelandfire.gov.uk

CORNWALL COUNTY FIRE BRIGADE
Old County Hall
Station Road
Truro
TR1 3HA
Tel. 01872 273117
www.cornwall.gov.uk/fire

CUMBRIA COUNTY FIRE SERVICE
Station Road
Cockermouth
CA13 9PR
Tel. 01900 822503
www.cumbriafire.gov.uk

DERBYSHIRE FIRE AND RESCUE SERVICE
The Old Hall
Burton Road
Littleover
Derbyshire
DE23 6EH
Tel. 01332 771221
www.derbyshire-fire-service.co.uk

DEVON FIRE AND RESCUE
The Knowle
Clyst St George
Exeter
EX3 0NW
Tel. 01392 872200
www.devfire.gov.uk

DORSET FIRE AND RESCUE SERVICE
Colliton Park
Dorchester
Dorset
DT1 1FB
Tel. 01305 251133
www.dorsetfire.gov.uk

DUMFRIES AND GALLOWAY FIRE BRIGADE
Brooms Road
Dumfries
DG1 2DZ
Tel. 01387 252222
www.dumgal.gov.uk

DURHAM AND DARLINGTON FIRE AND RESCUE
Framwellgate Moor
Durham
DH1 5JR
Tel. 0191 384 3381
www.ddfra.co.uk

EAST SUSSEX FIRE AND RESCUE SERVICE
Headquarters
20 Upperton Road
Eastbourne
East Sussex
BN21 1EU
Tel. 08451 308855
www.esfrs.org

ESSEX COUNTY FIRE AND RESCUE SERVICE
Rayleigh Close
Rayleigh Road
Hutton
Brentwood
Essex
CM13 1AL
Tel. 01277 222531
www.essex-fire.gov.uk

FIFE FIRE AND RESCUE SERVICE
Strathore Road
Thornton
Kirkcaldy
Fife
KY1 4DF
Tel. 01592 774451
www.fifefire.gov.uk

GLOUCESTERSHIRE FIRE AND RESCUE
Waterwells Drive
Quedgeley
Gloucestershire
GL2 2AX
Tel. 01452 753333
www.glosfire.gov.uk

GRAMPIAN FIRE AND RESCUE SERVICE
19 North Anderson Drive
Aberdeen
AB15 6TP
Tel. 01224 696666
www.grampianfirebrigade.co.uk

GREATER MANCHESTER FIRE AND RESCUE SERVICE
146 Bolton Road
Swinton
Manchester
M27 8US
Tel. 0161 736 5866
www.manchesterfire.gov.uk

GUERNSEY FIRE BRIGADE
Town Arsenal
St Peter Port
Guernsey
GY1 1UW
Tel. 01481 724491
www.gov.gg/ccm/navigation/home-department/fire-service

HAMPSHIRE FIRE AND RESCUE SERVICE
Leigh Road
Eastleigh
Hampshire
SO50 9SJ
Tel. 023 8064 4000
www.hantsfire.gov.uk

HEREFORD AND WORCESTER FIRE AND RESCUE SERVICE
2 Kings Court
Charles Hastings Way
Worcester
WR5 1JR
Tel. 08451 224454
www.hwfire.org.uk

HERTFORDSHIRE FIRE AND RESCUE SERVICE
Old London Road
Hertford
SG13 7LD
Tel. 01992 507601
www.hertsdirect.org/yrccouncil/hcc/fire

HIGHLANDS AND ISLANDS FIRE BRIGADE
Harbour Road
Longman West
Inverness
IV1 1TB
Tel. 01463 227000
www.hifb.org

HUMBERSIDE FIRE AND RESCUE SERVICE
Brigade Headquarters
Summergroves Way
Hessle High Road
Hull
HU4 7BB
Tel. 01482 565333
www.humbersidefire.gov.uk

ISLE OF MAN FIRE AND RESCUE SERVICE
Fire Service Headquarters
Elm Tree House
Elm Tree Road
Onchan
Isle of Man
IM3 4EF
Tel. 01624 647300
www.iomfire.com

ISLES OF SCILLY FIRE BRIGADE
Fire Brigade Administration Centre
The Airport, St Marys
Isles of Scilly
TR21 0NG
Tel. 01720 422677
www.scilly.gov.uk/transport/airandsea/airport/fireandrescue.htm

ISLE OF WIGHT FIRE AND RESCUE SERVICE
St Nicholas
58 St Johns Road
Newport
Isle of Wight
PO30 1LT
Tel. 01983 823194
www.iwfire.org.uk

JERSEY FIRE AND RESCUE SERVICE
Fire Service Headquarters
PO Box 509
Rouge Bouillon
St Helier
JE2 3ZA
Tel. 01534 633506
www.gov.je/homeaffairs/fire

KENT FIRE BRIGADE
The Godlands
Tovil
Maidstone
Kent
ME15 6XB
Tel. 01622 692121
www.kent.fire-uk.org

LANCASHIRE FIRE AND RESCUE
Garstang Road
Fulwood
Preston
PR2 3LH
Tel. 01772 862545
www.lancsfirerescue.org.uk

LEICESTERSHIRE FIRE AND RESCUE SERVICE
Anstey Frith
Leicester Road
Glenfield
Leicester
LE3 8HD
Tel. 0116 287 2241
www.leicestershire-fire.gov.uk

LINCOLNSHIRE FIRE AND RESCUE
South Park Avenue
Lincoln
LN5 8EL
Tel. 01522 582200
www.lincolnshirefire.org.uk

LONDON FIRE BRIGADE
8 Albert Embankment
London
SE1 7SD
Tel. 020 7587 2000
www.london-fire.gov.uk

LOTHIAN AND BORDERS FIRE BRIGADE
Lauriston Place
Edinburgh
EH3 9DE
Tel. 0131 228 2401
www.lothian.fire-uk.org

MERSEYSIDE FIRE AND RESCUE SERVICE
Bridle Road
Bootle
Merseyside
L30 4YD
Tel. 0151 296 4000
www.merseyfire.gov.uk

MID AND WEST WALES FIRE BRIGADE
Fire Brigade Headquarters
Lime Grove Avenue
Carmarthen
SA31 3SP
Tel. 0870 606 0699
www.mawwfire.gov.uk

NORFOLK FIRE SERVICE
Whitegates
Hethersett
Norwich
NR9 3DN
Tel. 01603 810351
www.norfolkfireservice.gov.uk

NORTHAMPTONSHIRE FIRE AND RESCUE SERVICE
Moulton Way
Moulton Park
Northampton
NN3 6XJ
Tel. 01604 797000
http://www.northamptonshire.gov.uk/safety/fire

NORTHUMBERLAND FIRE AND RESCUE SERVICE
Loansdean
Morpeth
Northumberland
NE61 2ED
Tel. 01670 533000
www.northumberland.gov.uk/cs_fire.asp

NORTH YORKSHIRE FIRE BRIGADE
Thurston Road
Northallerton
DL6 2ND
Tel. 01609 780150
www.northyorksfire.gov.uk

NORTHERN IRELAND FIRE AUTHORITY
6 Bankmore Street
Belfast
BT7 1AQ
Tel. 028 9031 0360
www.nifrs.org

NORTH WALES FIRE SERVICE
Ffordd Salesbury
St Asaph Business Park
St Asaph
LL17 0JJ
Tel. 01745 535250
www.nwales-fireservice.org.uk

NOTTINGHAMSHIRE FIRE AND RESCUE SERVICE
Bestwood Lodge
Arnold
Nottingham
NG5 8PD
Tel. 0115 967 0880
www.notts-fire.gov.uk

OXFORDSHIRE FIRE SERVICE
Sterling Road
Kidlington
Oxford
OX5 2DU
Tel. 01865 842999
www.oxfordshire.gov.uk/fire_service

ROYAL BERKSHIRE FIRE AND RESCUE SERVICE
103 Dee Road
Tilehurst
Reading
RG30 4FS
Tel. 0118 945 2888
www.rbfrs.co.uk

SHROPSHIRE FIRE AND RESCUE SERVICE
St Michaels Street
Shrewsbury
Shropshire
SY1 2HJ
Tel. 01743 260200
www.shropshirefire.gov.uk

SOMERSET FIRE BRIGADE
Hestercombe House
Cheddon Fitzpaine
Taunton
TA2 8LQ
Tel. 01823 364603
www.somersetfirebrigade.co.uk

SOUTH WALES FIRE SERVICE
Lanelay Hall
Pontyclun
Mid Glamorgan
CF72 9XA
Tel. 01443 232000
www.southwales-fire.gov.uk

SOUTH YORKSHIRE FIRE AND RESCUE
Command Headquarters
Wellington Street
Sheffield
S1 3FG
Tel. 0114 272 7202
www.syfire.org.uk

STAFFORDSHIRE FIRE AND RESCUE SERVICE
Pirehill
Stone
Staffordshire
ST15 0BS
Tel. 08451 221155
www.staffordshirefire.gov.uk

STRATHCLYDE FIRE BRIGADE
Bothwell Road
Hamilton
Lanarkshire
ML3 0EA
Tel. 01698 300999
www.strathclydefire.org

SUFFOLK COUNTY FIRE SERVICE
Colchester Road
Ipswich
Suffolk
IP4 4SS
Tel. 01473 588888
www.suffolkcc.gov.uk/fire

SURREY FIRE AND RESCUE SERVICE
St Davids
70 Wray Park Road
Reigate
RH2 0EJ
Tel. 01737 242444
www.surreycc.gov.uk

TAYSIDE FIRE BRIGADE
Fire Brigade Headquarters
Blackness Road
Dundee
DD1 5PA
Tel. 01382 322222
www.taysidefire.gov.uk

TYNE AND WEAR FIRE AND RESCUE SERVICE
Nissan Way
Washington
SR5 3QY
Tel. 0191 444 1500
www.twfire.org

WARWICKSHIRE FIRE AND RESCUE
Warwick Street
Royal Leamington Spa
Warwickshire
CV32 5LH
Tel. 01926 423231
www.warwickshire.gov.uk/fireandrescue

WEST MIDLANDS FIRE SERVICE
Lancaster Circus
Queensway
Birmingham
B4 7DE
Tel. 0121 380 7404
www.wmfs.net

WEST SUSSEX FIRE BRIGADE
Northgate
Chichester
West Sussex
PO19 1BD
Tel. 01243 786211
www.wsfb.co.uk

WEST YORKSHIRE FIRE SERVICE
Oakroyd Hall
Birkenshaw
Bradford
BD11 2DY
Tel. 01274 682311
www.westyorksfire.gov.uk

WILTSHIRE AND SWINDON FIRE AUTHORITY
Manor House
Potterne
Devizes
SN10 5PP
Tel. 01380 723601
www.wfb.org.uk